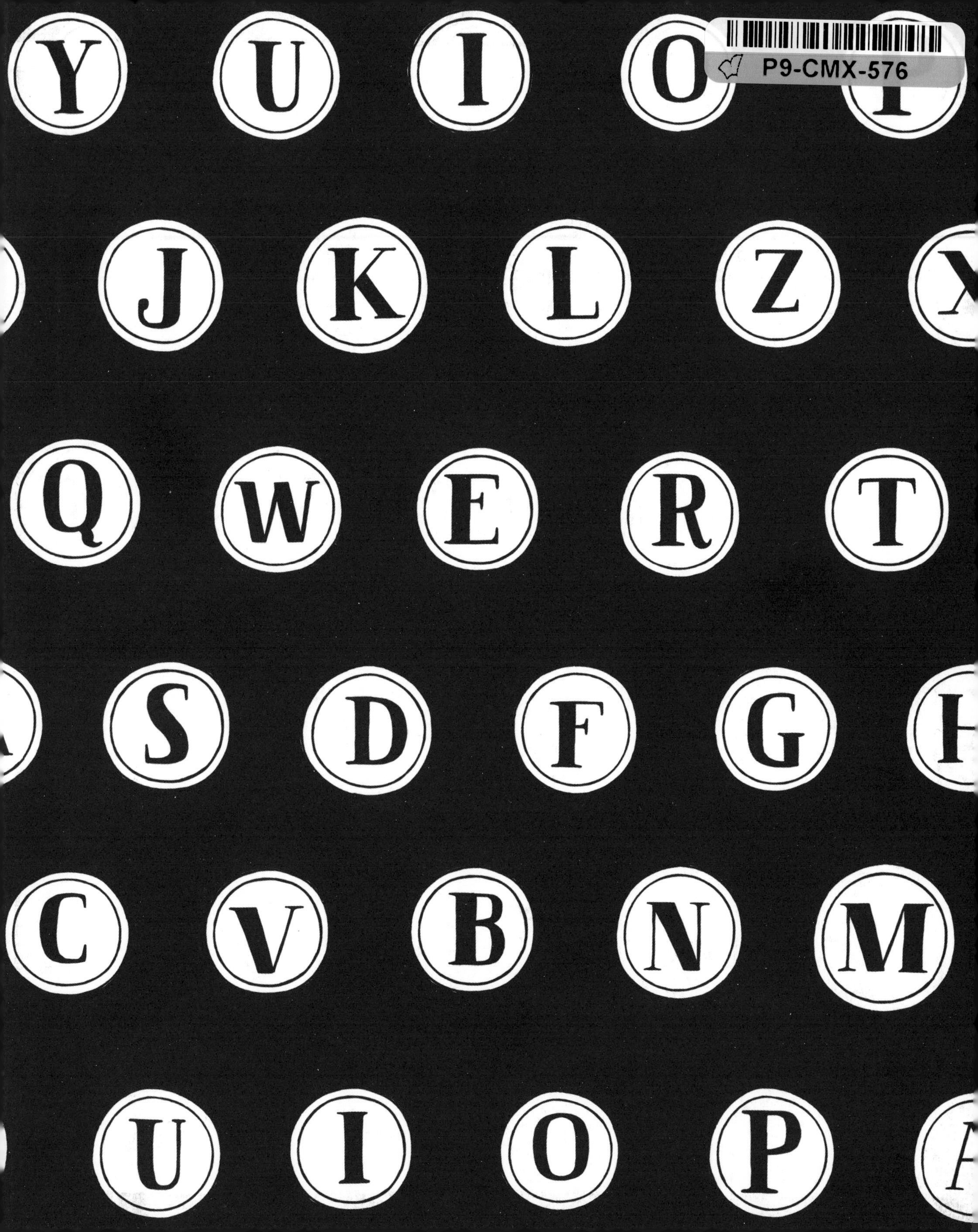
Y U I O
J K L Z
Q W E R T
S D F G
C V B N M
U I O P

Little People, **BIG DREAMS**

AGATHA CHRISTIE

Written by
Mª Isabel Sánchez Vegara

Illustrated by
Elisa Munsó

Translated by Raquel Plitt

**Frances Lincoln
Children's Books**

Little Agatha and her mother read a book together every afternoon. Agatha always had a better idea for how the story should end!

IV Sherlock Holmes

In bed, Agatha kept on reading until she fell asleep. Detective novels were her favorite.

But then a war started, and young Agatha had to put her books aside. It was time for her to help wounded soldiers in a hospital.

But Agatha's imagination wouldn't stay quiet. As a nurse, she learned about poisons and toxic potions, which could cause someone to meet an unfortunate end.

After the war, Agatha used what she had learned to write her own stories. They always started with a mysterious murder. Who could solve such terrible crimes?

The Love of Beauty

Agatha invented Hercule Poirot, a detective able to decipher any dastardly deed!

Carrying her typewriter, Agatha traveled the world. People read with wonder as Poirot solved crime after crime.

ORIENT EXPRESS

Agatha reached the Middle East, where she was inspired to write a mystery that Poirot couldn't crack.

DEATH ON THE NILE

So she invented Miss Marple to take the case!
She looked more like a granny than a detective . . .
But Agatha knew that appearances
could be deceiving.

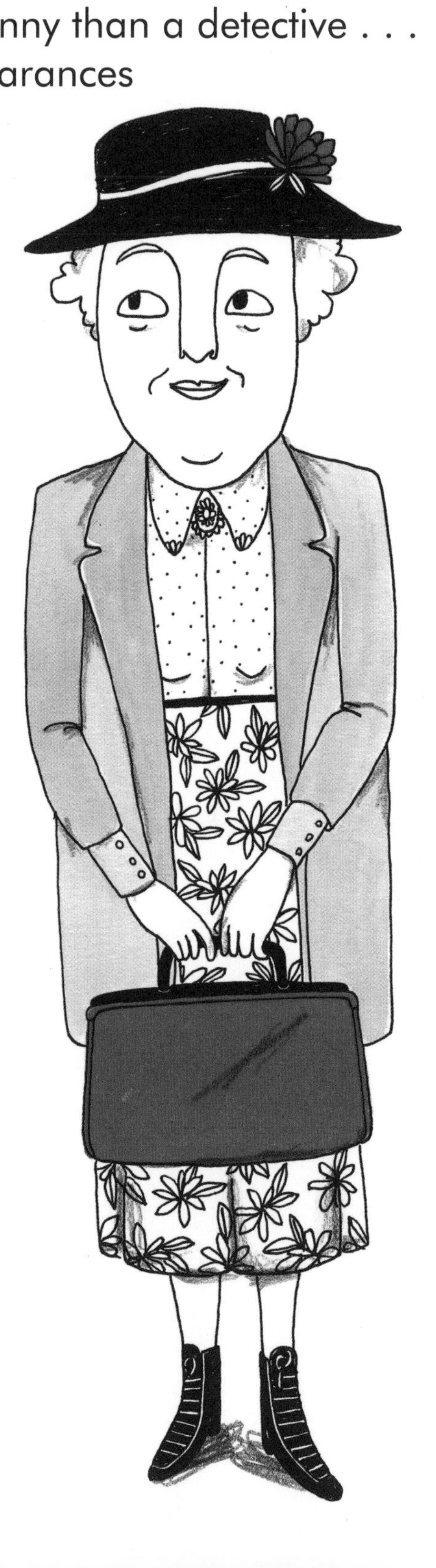

L.TD SHOE REBUILDER L.TD SHOE

And soon everyone loved Miss Marple as much as Poirot. They read Agatha's adventures before going to bed . . .

. . . and gulped and gasped at them in the theater.

Aristide Leonides
1949
Louise Leidner
1936
Mr. Ratchett
1934
Linnet Ridgeway
1937
Colonel
Lucius
Protheroe
1930
Fenella
Guteman
1967
Mr & Mrs
Rogers
1939

Agatha wrote more than a hundred books and invented enough victims to fill a cemetery! But she was always pondering her next mystery . . .

Death in the Clouds
A murder is Announced
NEMESIS
DEATH COMES AS THE END
Crooked House
THE MAN IN THE BROWN SUIT
FIVE LITTLE PIGS
MURDER ON THE ORIENT EXPRESS
A Caribbean Mystery
Evil Under the Sun
AND THEN THERE WERE NONE
AFTER the FUNERAL
The murder at the Vicarage
The murder of Roger Ackroyd
4:50 from Paddington
THE MYSTERIOUS AFFAIR AT STYLES
The Secret Adversary
THE ABC MURDERS
CARDS ON THE TABLE
APPOINTMENT with DEATH

Luckily, Agatha knew that any mystery can be solved if you use your imagination.

AGATHA CHRISTIE

(Born 1890 • Died 1976)

c. 1900

1926

Agatha Christie was born Agatha Mary Chrissie Miller in 1890 in Devon, England. During the war, Agatha worked as a nurse and also dispensed medicines at the hospital. Her new expertise in poisons was put to good use when she began writing her own detective stories. In 1919, a publisher accepted *The Mysterious Affair at Styles* for publication, which was the first novel to feature the famous detective Hercule Poirot. An avid traveler, in 1922 she journeyed across the British Empire, and in 1928 she was inspired by her journey on the Orient Express to write one of her most famous novels: *Murder on the Orient Express*. In 1925, Agatha inspired her own

1946

1967

mystery when she disappeared, leading to a nationwide hunt! She was eventually found safe and sound in a hotel. As time went on, Agatha continued to write, inventing her other beloved investigator, the elderly Miss Marple. Agatha Christie became the best-selling novelist of all time. Her books have been translated into more than a hundred languages and her novel *And Then There Were None* is one of the ten most-read books in history. With her peculiar characters, her enigmatic cases, and her stories full of twists and turns, she challenged the minds of millions of readers, becoming the queen of mystery.

First published in the USA in 2017 by Frances Lincoln Children's Books,
74–77 White Lion Street, London N1 9PF, UK
QuartoKnows.com
Visit our blogs at QuartoKnows.com

First published in Spain in 2016 under the title *Pequeña & Grande Agatha Christie*
by Alba Editorial, s.l.u.
Baixada de Sant Miquel, 1, 08002 Barcelona
www.albaeditorial.es

UK ISBN 978-1-84780-960-5

Printed in China

3 5 7 9 8 6 4 2

Photographic acknowledgments (pages 28–29, from left to right) 1. Agatha Christie as a young girl, c. 1900 © The Christie Archive Trust
2. Agatha Christie in 1926 © Bettman, Getty Images 3. Agatha Christie at a typewriter in her home in Devonshire, 1946 © Bettman, Getty
Images 4. Portrait of English mystery writer Agatha Christie, 1967 © Underwood Archives, Getty Images

Also in the *Little People*, **BIG DREAMS** series:

FRIDA KAHLO

ISBN: 978-1-84780-783-0

Frida Kahlo's terrible childhood accident did not stop her from being one of the best artists of the twentieth century.

COCO CHANEL

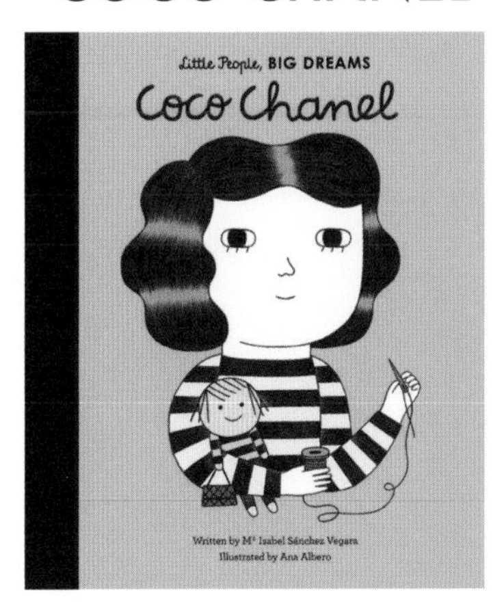

ISBN: 978-1-84780-784-7

Coco Chanel was a cabaret singer, hat-maker, seamstress, and one of the most famous fashion designers that has ever lived.

MAYA ANGELOU

ISBN: 978-1-84780-889-9

After a traumatic event at age eight, Maya Angelou discovered her voice and went on to become one of the world's most beloved writers.

AMELIA EARHART

ISBN: 978-1-84780-888-2

Amelia Earhart's strong will, hard work, and self-belief helped her to become the first female aviator to fly solo across the Atlantic.

MARIE CURIE

ISBN: 978-1-84780-962-9

Marie Curie's love of knowledge led her to make huge discoveries in the fight against cancer, and win the Nobel Prize for Physics.

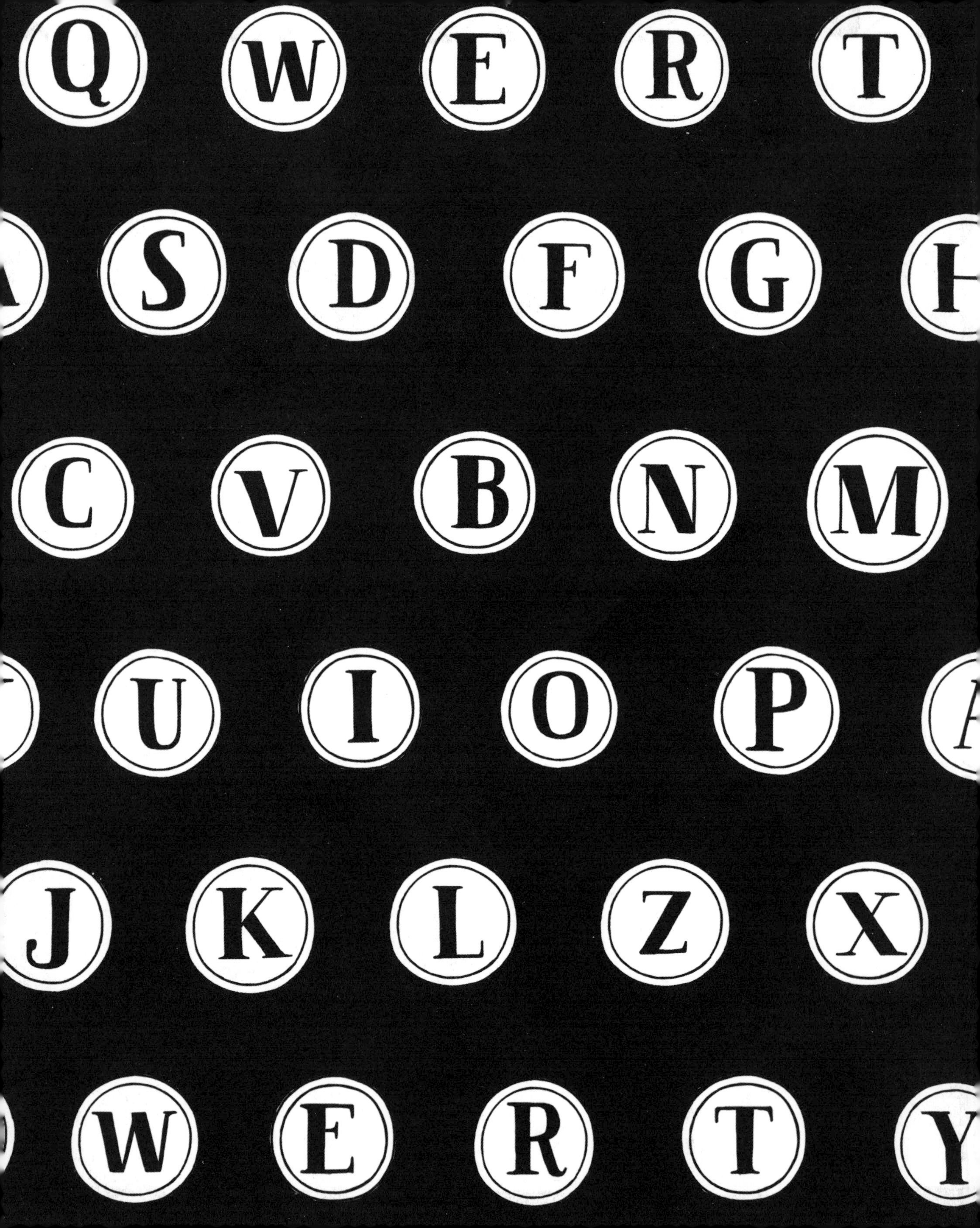
Q W E R T
S D F G
C V B N M
U I O P
J K L Z X
W E R T